Echoes

Mahek Parmar

BookLeaf
Publishing

India | USA | UK

Dedication

To my parents, who laid the foundation for my dreams and whose love is the thread that weaves through every page of this book. To my mother, whose spirit continues to guide me, her love echoing in every word I write.

Preface

Explore the echoes within the walls of different rooms, where emotions reverberate and stories bloom. From the comfort of homecoming to the introspective depths of self-awareness, each poem invites readers to discover the chambers of being a human in 'Echoes'.

Acknowledgements

I would like to thank my lovely family for being the echoes of my creativity. I would also like to express my heartfelt gratitude to all my dearest friends for their grateful support, encouragement, and inspiration throughout the process of bringing this book to life. They have been a source of strength and inspiration, filling the pages of my life with laughter, love, and cherished memories. Thank you all for being the pillars of support in the tapestry of my existence.

Home

Turn the key, hear the squeaky push of the door,
Familiar scents embrace, a few to explore
Sun kisses the face, a warm caress,
Walls hold stories unaddressed.

The wardrobe's anger creaks
Every day's attention it seeks
Dust settles softly on the desk,
Counting days since it took rest.

Painting still unmoved an inch,
Reassures, none disturbed a pinch.
Whispers of laughter and tears that fly,
Each room holds echoes of days gone by.

This feeling, this comfort, deeply known,
Ladies and gentlemen, what it means to be home.

Warp and Weft Room

Between destiny's tangled thread,
Hopes are spun, fears are shed.
Every twist, every snare,
A burden in life's complex lair.

Every dawn, a knot to untie,
But if dreams came true with no try,
If wishes were granted without a fight,
Would we ever cherish the light?

Retangle thoughts from days long gone,
Realizing, the knots we once shunned are now our own.
Just as we've learned to knot through strife,
We knit our path in this tangled life.

Each tangle, a thread to weave,
In chaos, the needle deceives,
Creating beauty from every mess,
Stitching our stories, we must confess.

So here's a toast to life's tangled art,
To weaving tales with every knot.
On destiny's ground, we knit and press,
Raise your cup, "to the mess."

The Hall of Seasons

Let's talk about seasons,
It's nature shaping our rhythms.
While summer thirsts for the rain's cool,
Fall, yearns for its blooms.

Summer gathers sweat like a hardworking artisan,
Crafting clouds for the sky's grand plan.
Winter sculpts frost's delicate lace,
As spring orchestrates nature's embrace.

Each season tells a nature-tale
Exchanging secrets/ tricks, it plays its game
While we start to glow with warmth at the dusk of cold
Golden fields prepare to whisper, "may" the daffodils feel
less alone.

It's the nature's nature to ace it with grace
From growing April to falling snow
Perhaps autumn exists to prepare us for the December's
chill,
A gentle transition, nature's serene skill.

A Living Room

Memories, like CDs stored on a rack,
Mom's gossip, Dad's jokes, Grandparent's cute
bickering.
Each of us holds a version, uniquely our own,
Highlighting the hall with the love we've known.

The hierarchy of family, a timeless array,
Roles and seats, never changing, always in play.
Whether you sit on the sofa or crawl around its frame,
These memories are the seats in our hearts, where love
remains.

As we build our worlds, near or apart,
These moments will be the places we revisit and restart.
In the living room of our minds, forever clear,
We'll sit and smile, holding those we hold dear.

Room for an Extra Platter

I wished you'd meet me at my silent shore,
Where the waves of my soul softly roar,
Where I, me, and myself reside,
In a place where thoughts and feelings collide.

But you found me there,
Delved into deep conversations with care,
Unveiling the crockery hidden for years,
Staying through the darkest hour of my fears.

I thought it hard to let you stay,
But you tore down walls, showed the way
To peace within, where tides run serene,
Your embrace breaks through the scene.

Dining each day with an extra platter
Became my routine, nothing else mattered.
When emptiness stayed,
Your fragrance was all I craved.

I wished you'd meet me at the silent shore,
But fate had something more in store.
You came as a tourist passing by,
Now an extra platter and anchor mine.

A Bedroom

I never realized it was a well-decorated blank canvas,
A diary where silent thoughts find streams.
Outside the door, a mask calm and seamless,
Inside, pillows cradle my muffled dreams.

In this room, two faces come alive,
One for the world, one where true thoughts thrive.
Mind, words and their nightly silent war,
Heart the judge, poetry the law.

Here, the walls hold whispers, not heard by day,
Secrets shared in shadows, where they lay.
In this sanctuary, I find my truest self,
A place where my soul can speak, and nothing else.

The Observation Deck

Isn't it obvious?
When he plays with her hair,
Pulls out her chair,
He's in love, or so we declare.

When she blushes,
Every time his name is called,
Her heart must race
But is it love, or just the chase?

Isn't it obvious?
When best friends share everything,
Despite the cracks,
Society mistrusts their lack.

Isn't it obvious?
When jealousy flares,
Insecurity paired,
They stay together, but do they care?

Isn't it obvious?
When apologies are made,
Ego set aside
Yet true feelings may still hide.

*

But why must love be well-defined,
Actions so neatly aligned?
Why are disputes left to grow,
And arguments allowed to slow?

The obvious isn't always truth,
It's shaped by norms that we construe.
We see what we're taught to find,
Not the heart, but the social mind.

Obvious isn't just displayed,
It's a script we've all replayed.
In gestures seen, meanings imposed,
But real love often goes unexposed.

Library

People are libraries, where whispers reside,
Each life a book, with stories inside.
Volumes unique, each in their way,
With tales to tell, and lessons to convey.

Every individual, a book to explore,
With chapters of life, and much more instore.
In humanity's library, vast and grand,
Each heart holds a tale, every soul a plan.

Playground

The playgrounds that yelled "1,2,3,4..."
Where we played and friendships soared.
Now, memories trapped in a digital frame,
Lost to Player Unknown's Battlegrounds (PUBG) game.

Exams meant group study, bonds tight,
Now Zoom calls replace those nights.
Textbooks were once shared, now screens reign,
Connection reduced to virtual strain.

We'd wait for the ice cream cart's chime,
Summer cousins, friends perfect time.
Now, Instagram requests and like-clicks replaced the
joyful quest,
Trapped in frames, we lose the rest.

From open fields to virtual bounds,
Play and connection, silent grounds.
In the frames where we once ran free,
Now lies a world of virtuality.

The Garden of Reflection

In the garden's calm, where flowers sway,
One choice away, to greet the day.
With a whispering breeze, a path unfolds,
One choice away, where change takes hold.

With each seed planted, the earth understands,
One choice away, change begins, as seeds expand.
In the garden's serenity, dreams take flight,
One choice away, to break the cocoon, to fly.

So listen close, to your dream's song,
Change beckons, where happiness belong.
In every petal, a whisper of chance,
In every leaf, a hopeful dance.

For every day, Remember to water your dreams,
Nurture them with hope's gentle streams.
Change is but one decision away,
A shift in perspective, come what may.

The Clock Room

I've asked Time a question or two:
Does it pass in a beat, or moments anew?
Is time a friend or foe,
Or just a lens through which we view?

Does it delay when we yearn for more,
Or rush ahead when we implore?
Do we fear its rules in command,
Or does it slip away, once we understand?

Time whispered back, soft and clear,
"Perhaps I'm a cog in life's gear.
While you ponder, I simply move,
Forgetting I wait for none to approve."

And so I learned:
Time carves paths where obstacles stood firm.
It scripts life's tale,
With each turn of its kale.

So whether kind or harsh its decree,
Whether it stays or swiftly flees,
It demands respect, a reverence due,
For time's the clock that shapes our view.

Nursery

One, two, you buckled our shoes,
Lacing our lives in your love's infinity loop.
Twinkle, twinkle, oh Mom, I wonder what you are,
Guiding us ever, like a steadfast pole star.

Teaching steady steps, like Jack and Jill,
With carrots and sticks, so we'd never tumble a hill.
You sang "Johnny, Johnny," in tones so clear,
Instilling in us truth, with no trace of fear.

From the world, you took Humpty's great fall,
Gathered the pieces, mended us all.
Oh Mom! in the cacoon of your arms we grew,
Shaped by the love that only you knew.

The Yellow Room

Have you ever felt yellow? Strange to say,
We feel blue, go red, turn green and even grey
But yellow, burst of crazy and bright,
Positive and warm, like the morning light.

In today's world, feeling yellow's a treasure,
A mark of good mental health, pure pleasure.
Realising it, understanding its glow,
Makes you want the world to bask in its flow.

Yellow tempts us to spread joy, to start,
With tiny steps, we share our heart.
A positive mind does wonders, it's true,
Creating self-awareness, a broader view.

The Makeup Room

Your lips that strain to smile,
Why not frown and cry for a while?
The concealer beneath your eye,
Whispers, am I just a lie?

Ears poised to hear,
"No worries, I'm here, all ears."
Your eyes unblinking, awaiting another's glance,
To see past the fake blush.

Release the wrinkles and pain,
Fill with courage to face the anguish again.
But where has your courage gone?
What makes you wear that enforced dawn?

Why do I, your makeup, question my role,
And why do your senses lose their goal?
Where pain is meant to be felt,
And tears are meant to be shed,

Why must happiness alone
Be the mask that's always shown?

The Terrace

Trapped in cages of love and grudges tightly bound,
One deep breath and freedom is found.
Close your eyes and Inhale....
feel the air rush in,

Breaking chains of doubt, releasing within.
Exhale ....slow, let the worries fade away,
Feel yourself soar high, in the light of day.
Feel the world beneath and vast sky,

Inhale the peace
and exhale the sigh.

Cooking Empathy

A recipe for connection with each step we take,
In the kitchen of hearts, where healing we bake.
With empathy as our secret, our guiding light,
We stir a world where understanding takes flight.

8

Let's begin our brew,
With care, compassion and understanding too.
Gather the ingredients emotions in a mix,
Blend them with kindness, for an empathetic fix.

Start with a dash of patience, a pinch of grace,
Fold in listening, at a steady pace.
Add a dollop of comfort, a sprinkle of cheer,
Simmer with questions, until emotions are clear.

Slice through doubts, chop misunderstandings away,
Knead in some smiles to brighten the day.
Inside, a stew of feelings, tender and true,
Outside, the warmth of positive-tea brews.

Like a kitchen's dance, precise and sweet,
An empathetic healing, ready to greet.
Let it simmer on the stove of the heart,
Till it's ready to serve, a work of art.

Aurora Lounge

In the stillness of night, from my bedroom's embrace,
I gazed out the window, lost in its grace.
The northern lights danced, right outside my door,
A marvel I'd sought, but fate brought to my shore.

For years, I dreamed of this celestial fire,
To witness its glow, to feel its desire.
I planned to journey to far-off lands,
But the universe placed it within my hands.

Unbidden it came, in the quiet night's frame,
A wonder so grand, it couldn't be tamed.
It painted joy where shadows had been,
A gift of the cosmos, a light within.

I ponder still, how it found its way,
To my window, where dreams often stray.
Such is the magic of life's subtle cues,
Guiding us gently with cosmic hues.

The Room of Contrast

If there is no bad,
What is good?
If it's not awful,
How will it be wonderful?

If nothing's disgusting,
How can something be charming?
If there are no villains,
Who will define heroes?

If nothing is dumb,
Can we be smart?
If there is no 'right,'
There is also nothing 'not right.'

If there is no humane,
There is nothing inhumane.
Everything has a reason to exist, and,
Nothing in this world can be dismissed.
Balance gives life its meaning.

Storeroom of Identity

That smile fades when our eyes meet,
"Long time, let's catch up!" we repeat.
Red lipstick to hide the blues,
Joining the crowd, it's just what we do.

Polished small talk to ease the guilt,
That fancy accent to match the image we built.
Pulling out chairs, playing the part,
Pampering ourselves to mask the heart.

Maybe we're all just trying to show respect,
But maybe… it's not what we expect.
What's needed are genuine smiles,
Turning texts into shared miles.

Lipstick that matches how we feel,
Knowing expression won't conceal.
Honest words in conversation,
Laughing at our own hesitation.

Shedding obligations, free from the norm,
Pampering ourselves, embracing the storm.
We meet expectations, show respect,
But maybe… just maybe, it's time to reflect.

The Realm of Self

We understand but don't always realize,
Two notions so close, yet worlds apart.
Realization is the first step, a gentle rise,
To truly know, to the heart from the start.

Self-awareness is the key, the silent guest,
To make sense of who we are, to set us free.
Understanding comes with ease for others' plight,
But self-understanding, a harder art to grasp.

If unspoken words from others stir our mind,
How much more do our own unsaid thoughts confine?
To leave things unsaid to oneself, we find,
Is to be trapped within, misaligned.

Simple Joys

When we had a small house, walls close in tight,
Either there is no privacy or electricity, the only
problems at night.
With problems shared, solutions found fast,
Everyone was accessible, we stood tall.

Exotic cuisines? No, just one dish to savour,
Waiting together, our bonds grew bigger.
No individual tastes, no need to choose,
In our small house, unity we'd infuse.

Though space was limited,
In our small house, where we all did belong.
For in its walls, love was the glue,
Uniting us in all we did.

Small house, small problems, but hearts ran deep,
In its humble embrace, love never denied.
For in our tiny haven, we found our bliss,
In each other's company, blessing it is.

Milton Keynes UK
Ingram Content Group UK Ltd.
UKHW030758121124
451094UK00014B/1086

9 789363 300378